LOST ANGEL
in PARADISE

Great Outdoor Days from Los Angeles to the Lost Coast

LINDA BALLOU

Lost Angel in Paradise, Great Outdoor Days from Los Angeles to the Lost Coast of California, copyright 2019 by Linda Ballou

Published by Wind Dancer Press
Cover by Alexandria Corza
Images by Linda Ballou
Layout by www.formatting4U.com

WHAT READERS ARE SAYING

"As a lover of hiking and LA myself, I have found my nirvana. Thank you Linda Ballou for giving us this gift."

~Dr. Skyler Madison, The Creative Writer's Way

"Linda Ballou's travel writing has provided me with hours of captivated reading. I loved her book *Lost Angel Walkabout* which I could not put down until I finished it. Now, she blessed us with *Lost Angel in Paradise* and her angelic stories about hiking along the sun-splashed Californian coast from Malibu to Mendocino. I have done some of these hikes many years ago and to now read her colorful interpretation of these hikes is pure bliss!"

~Peter Steyn, Editor, *Globerovers Magazine*

"Lost Angel in Paradise is A GREAT tool for living in, or travel to, Los Angeles and along the beautiful Pacific coast. Linda Ballou, an experienced hiker and outdoorswoman, writes so beautifully, with lovely descriptions and photos of the amazing hikes few tourists or locals discover. Reading it, I felt that I knew she was there and she was describing each place and the many different kinds of hikes, from beach and island to mountaintops so poetically that it entices me to go!"

~Review by Bonnie Neely, Founder of
Real Travel Adventures Magazine

"Now you can delight in day-tripping adventures along with adventure travel writer Linda Ballou, who's long been known for her enticing articles about her power-packed outdoor days along the sun-splashed California coast from Malibu to Mendocino. For years, Linda's many friends have asked her if they could come with her on these adventures, and she's always declined. Not because she is unwilling to share, of course, but because, for Linda—as for many of us—a big part of the pleasure of the trip comes from the experience of solitary hiking. And yet, as powerful as solo trekking is, if you're heading off to somewhere you've never been before, we all know it's great to travel with a guide—especially if you're venturing off to new places. Which is why—if you're considering any day trips along the California Coast from Los Angeles to the Lost Coast—you can now take Linda along with you. Not in person. But the next best thing—a Kindle-formatted book with an app. (So Linda Ballou is talking to you, at your convenience, from your smart phone.)"

~Anne Holmes, CEO of The National Association
of Baby Boomer Women, www.nabbw.com

Table of Contents

Not All Who Wander Are Lost

Introduction

I have lived in California most of my life, but I am still a tourist, discovering new sweet spots along the coast—and loving it even more. I have explored hikes from Los Angeles to the Lost Coast north of Mendocino, taking in the Central and Northern Coast highlights along the way. In *Lost Angel in Paradise,* I take you to my favorite day hikes and beach walks along the Pacific, followed with directions to sweatband-friendly eateries close by. Days are laced with historical tidbits, notes about flora and fauna, and choice local insights. Points north of Los Angeles up to Fort Bragg include stops in Ventura, Santa Barbara, Santa Cruz, Point Reyes, Point Lobos, the Russian River, and Russian Gulch.

Nature can be our salvation from the constant stimuli in our busy world. A walk in the woods or a stroll on the sands allows our minds to digest it all. Creative ideas and solutions to problems bubble up from the deep well of the subconscious. The sensuality of nature—rhythms and sounds of rolling surf, swaying tree limbs, and more— becomes the meditation. Being quiet allows one to listen to the birds, chortling creeks, and wind voices. The Navajo actively pursue the state of harmony in nature and with society and the spirit world. It is a state they call Hozho. The great thinkers of the world have told us to "Be Here Now." We are admonished and encouraged to be in the present, not fretting about the future, regretting the past, or longing for something that no longer exists. Hiking livens the senses and pulls us into the moment.

I reside in the middle of the largest urban preserve in the United States. The Santa Monica Mountains National Recreation area encompasses more than 150,000 acres of mountains and coastline in Ventura and Los Angeles counties. It is veined with a network of trails that traverse the mountains to the sea. Many of the outdoor days in this collection are in the Santa Monicas and are among my favorite beaches and trails. Sadly, the Woolsey Fire in 2018 scorched many of my favorite trails. I have replaced them with hikes further up the coast and made notes on the ones I believe will recover in a season. There are still many wonderful outdoor days to enjoy. I hope you will reap benefits from these wonderful walks in the paradise I call home.

I do not provide maps or specific details or directions to each trail, rather, I strive to give you an essence of the experience. There are links to online sources referenced in each piece. At the back of the book is a list of good hiking books with maps and many other hiking-related options for you to explore.

(1) A Day In The "Bu" - Where It All Begins

I hike the half mile around Malibu Lagoon to what is famously known as Surf Riders Beach. Barefoot surfers join me on the shade-less path, carrying their boards tucked under their arms or over their heads. Unzipped wet suits folded down on slim waists keep them halfway cool. These are real he-men, if you ask me. I wear sneakers for the trek and carry supplies of water and fruit for when I get dry.

I pass the half-submerged section of the trail where whoever oversaw the multi-million dollar redo of the lagoon did not consider high tidal action. Families pull wagons full of beach supplies: umbrellas, chairs, and food—lots and lots of food—while pushing strollers.

The beach is lined with sparsely-clad individuals from around the world. At the entrance to Malibu Lagoon State Park, I was

3

snagged by a couple of gay caballeros from Italy who wanted their picture taken by the park sign. Their English was sketchy, but, with some animated sign language, I got the drift. Pasty-white Germans are a common sighting. Middle Eastern accents abound. There are Japanese women wearing big-brimmed hats and bandanas like the kind cowboys wear when herding cattle. Children of all ethnic origins are delirious with joy from spending a day in the sea, no matter what language their parents speak. They squeal at the top of their little lungs and run in and out of the surf, dragging diapers full of sand.

The local girls are spread out on towels, belly down, wearing bikinis that leave nothing to the imagination. They dare to bare themselves to an intense sun that crisps them like fritters on the sand. There are always co-eds snapping cell phone pictures of one another practicing coquettish poses to share with their Facebook fans. Occasionally, a young man with six-pack abs and his body oiled to glistening perfection will be flexing for a photo shoot. One day, I witnessed one woman stripping flirtatiously to the camera, perhaps auditioning for an adult film. It is, after all, Malibu—home to the rich and famous and those who want to be.

Surfers of all ages and genders fly in and out of the waves in their black wetsuits, tempting the great white sharks rumored to be heading this way. I figure there are so many of them to be mistaken as seals—natural shark food—that they will have no interest in little ole me—the solo female in a purple rash-guard, sporting three-foot fins.

I swim in the calmer waters by the Malibu pier. Swells there can be quite strong when the tropical storms come up from Baja and send ten-foot waves curling to shore with a thunderous crescendo. I have been caught out in the monster waves and barely escaped their crashing on my head. Getting out of the water is difficult as the ocean sucks the pulsing water and everything and everyone in it back into its clutches. So far, I have been able to count the wave sets and survive. With lifeguards busy surveying all those bare bottoms, I don't have much hope that anyone will run in to save me.

After my swim, I lay content under my umbrella, hoping to avoid dying from melanoma, and watching the surfers fight to get the perfect take-off spot. I envy them their grace and agility, and marvel that some of them have survived long enough to collect social security. Once a surfer, always a surfer? Even the gray-hairs are wiry and fit. It's a good way to die.

The biggest challenge for me is getting a shady place to park. On those formidable-looking days, I go down Malibu Canyon Road to my favorite less-traveled beach where locals hang out and bring their dogs. It is a finable offense, but since there is no one to call them out for this transgression, all breeds are represented. They frolic wildly, tearing up and down the sand, sniffing freely of their fellows, and generally having a heck of a good time. So far, it has not been a problem for me, though I have had a few interlopers come to my marked-out territory on the sand to shake themselves vigorously, sending spray my way.

Summer in the "Bu" is busy for good reason. The water is a deep aquamarine with foaming white ribbons rolling along the shore. The temp is invigorating and it is hard to stay away, so I am heading back today. Not sure what I'll find, but it is always a heady way to while away an afternoon.

Malibu Lagoon State Beach
      www.parks.ca.gov/?page_id=835

(2) Adamson House - Malibu - Where The Surf Speaks Loudly

There is a sign posted that says, "Malibu Lagoon Museum," but the fast-moving traffic on Pacific Coast Highway does not encourage one to stop and explore the Adamson House behind the block wall covered in honeysuckle and bougainvillea. The Spanish hacienda, built in the '20s, was originally the beach home of the first family of Malibu. It rests on thirteen prime coastal acres overlooking Surf Riders Beach. Mrs. Adamson was the daughter of feisty Mae Rindge who once owned land from Topanga Canyon to the Ventura County line.

The Adamson's architects took full advantage of the vistas of the sparkling Pacific. Portholes were placed in the upstairs study to give Mr. Adamson the effect of being at sea. The home was procured by imminent domain by the state and spared the fate of becoming a parking lot because of the extensive use of the marvelous tiles throughout the home produced in Mae Rindge's tile factory. Electric blue accents in terra cotta tiles in the fountains and courtyard echo the blue of the sequined Pacific.

Mrs. Adamson had five full-time gardeners on staff to maintain the lush grounds bursting with blooms. A sunny bench overlooks the lagoon where thousands of birds congregate. Pelican, terns, herons, and egrets flock here in abundance. Environmental battles are not new to Malibu. Mrs. Rindge fought fiercely to keep the railroads and road-makers from making their tracks along the coast through her 17,500 acres of prime coastal land.

You can sit in the shade and watch the surfers sifting in and out of the foaming white rollers. Surfers come from around the globe to try their luck here. The waves can be as crowded as the Hollywood Freeway on a busy summer day. Even in the winter months, surfers bob like seals in the big blue, waiting for just the right wave to test their skills.

After a relaxing stroll through the Adamson grounds, walk about a block south to the entrance to Malibu Pier. The Malibu Farm eatery—where the infamous Alice's Restaurant once stood—overlooks the shore. A jazz trio in an outdoor cocktail lounge fills the air with cool tunes that say, "Come join me." More casual fare can be found on the tip of the pier in a more relaxed version of the Farm. I like the upstairs patio with the sea breeze and stunning views.

If you want to get inside the picture, you can rent a sea kayak or a paddle board in the parking lot next to the pier. I just take a swim in the calmest waters on the coast to the right of the pier.

The interior of the Adamson House is only visited with a guide, but visitors are invited to wander the manicured grounds from dawn until dusk. You can park in Surf Riders Beach parking lot which is owned by the county. Be sure to pay at the machines if no one is at the gate. The beach custodians are vigilant.

Adamson House
>www.adamsonhouse.org/

Surf Rider Beach
>www.beaches.lacounty.gov/malibu-surfrider-beach/

(3) Solstice Canyon - You Take The High Road And I'll Take The Low Road

Solstice Canyon has several trails with varying degrees of difficulty that take the hiker to one of few year-round waterfalls in the Santa Monica mountains. Follow the path tracing Solstice Creek and take the track on the right side of the bridge to Sun Rising Trail. After a quarter-mile ascent, you see a bright pool of sunshine glowing on the shimmering blue ocean far below. After winter rains, the canyon is bursting with blooms that include Indian paint brush, pink morning glory, blue dicks, and purple nightshade. New buds lift their faces to the warming sun, eager to join the spring bouquet. The Chumash Indians understood nature's ways and set fire to the hill, clearing the way for new life.

The high road levels off into an easy march across the top of the world. It descends to Tropical Terrace, the Roberts family's version of Shangri-La, once populated by exotic wildlife and destroyed by fire in 1982. All that remains is a fireplace and chimney. The gardens, with bird of paradise, palms, and other tropical plants, grow here in wild abandon at the base of the waterfall. A rock stairwell takes you to a pool lined with maidenhair ferns. Most people take the lower path (Sostomo Road) to approach the falls. It is easy enough for mothers with strollers and dog-walkers to enjoy. It follows the sycamore-shaded creek and takes Sun Rising Trail hikers back to the parking lot.

Close to the falls you will notice a fork that says, "Deer Trail Loop." That option is for those who need to feel the burn and would enjoy a sweeping view of Point Dume and want the chance to see a bit of wildlife. It is the least-traveled of the trails and, therefore, has its own special rewards... and dangers.

Solstice Creek is one of the few remaining places on the Southern California coastline that the endangered steelhead trout can swim upcreek to deposit their eggs. To remove barriers and make the creek fish-friendly cost the National Park Service about $1.5 million. Sadly, after five years of drought in California, I fear the creek is too shallow for the trout to survive.

Stop at the Malibu Seafood Café about a half-mile south of Corral Canyon, the entrance to the park, and enjoy the best fish and chips in Malibu. Then, take a stroll along the shore across from the cafe, or take a dip if you dare. There are lifeguards here in summer and dolphin arcing in the swells year-round.

Note: Solstice Canyon was damaged in the Woolsey Fire in 2018. It remains closed at this writing, but I believe it will be one of the first trails to be re-opened as it is one of the most scenic and popular in Malibu. Check with the park site below for current status.

Solstice Canyon
   www.nps.gov/samo/planyourvisit/solsticecanyon.htm

Malibu Seafood Café
   malibuseafood.com/

(4) The Point Dume - Bluff Trail

Hike up the well-traveled path that meanders though a meadow spiked with lupine and California poppies in the spring. In February, you will walk through mounds of brilliant yellow coreopsis, a shaggy form of rare daisy endemic to the region. Once aloft, enjoy majestic views of Windward Beach. If it looks familiar it is because it was used as the backdrop for the *Bay Watch* series and countless commercials. March on through deep, powdery sand to a ledge overlook where you might spy a lone fisherman, or a rock-climber repelling down the face of the promontory that frames Pirate's Cove. Continue to a wooden viewing platform jutting over the cliffs for a soul-stirring view of the coast and Santa Catalina Island. George Vancouver stopped here in 1776 and spoke of this uncompromised vista in his journal. In the winter months, "coastal" whales pass nearby on their annual 10,000-14,000 mile, round-trip migration from Alaska to the Pacific lagoons of Baja where they give birth to their young.

The last sweep of deserted sand in the scenic 27 miles of Malibu coast stretches out below, inviting the hiker to enjoy a bit of solitude. A pleasant wooden walkway takes the hardy to a dramatic 100-step stairwell, descending to what locals call the Malibu Riviera. At low tide, you can walk for miles below white cliffs draped in brilliant bougainvillea and bright magenta ice plant. Dolphin can be seen catching the waves that curl onshore while platoons of pelican swoop low over the water in search of a meal. Swimming here can be dangerous and is done without benefit of a lifeguard.

Time your walk to end at Sunset Café at the entrance to the Westward Beach parking lot. You can enjoy the tastiest fish tacos this side of the border while you watch the orange globe sink into the dark sea.

Another good choice is Spruzzo's which is upstairs in the little strip center nearby at 29575 Pacific Coast Highway. You have a nice view on the patio shaded by colorful umbrellas.

The trail begins where the Westward Beach county parking lot ends.

Note: There is free, two-hour parking for six cars on Cliffside Drive for the less energetic, but there is usually a long wait. Predatory parking enforcement prevails.

Point Dume State Beach
>   www.parks.ca.gov/?page_id=623

Sunset Restaurant
>   www.thesunsetrestaurant.com/

Spruzzo Restaurant
>   www.spruzzomalibu.com/

(5) Topanga State Park - Tried And True

Easily accessed from the San Fernando Valley as well as Santa Monica, Topanga State Park is a handy local favorite. Miles of trails radiate from the park center at the top of Entrada Road off of scenic Topanga Canyon Boulevard. The Musch trail meanders through oak woodlands and tree tunnels of mountain mahogany and California lilac to vistas of peaks framing the canyon below. You can take the Eagle Rock extension to this hike, then loop back to the park entrance on a fire road with views of Santa Monica Bay. Santa Ynez trail takes the ambitious hiker through dramatic rock formations to a creek lined with sycamore. The fire road that runs along the southern ridge is an easy march with majestic vistas of the glittering Pacific and Catalina Island on a clear day.

Archeological digs at the entrance to the park indicate that people have lived here in "climate-perfect" Topanga and used these trails from the mountain to the sea for 8,000 years. The Tongva people, dubbed Gabrielino by the Spanish, were not from the same root stock as the sea-faring Chumash tribe that populated villages along the coast. They spoke the Shoshone language and migrated along trade routes of the southwest native peoples. Stewards of the land, they groomed the vast grass meadows with controlled fires and trimmed the oaks to create the natural park setting they called home.

Deer grazing in the meadow are a common sighting. Yes, there are mountain lions here, but due to shrinking habitat, their numbers are waning. Coyotes are the most common predators. Always keep an eye out for rattlesnakes when hiking in the mountains. They usually give fair warning, but you can step on one sleeping by the side of trail if you are not vigilant. Mostly, you will see bushtits, hawks, and other birds on your outings.

Glide back down Entrada, make a left on Topanga Canyon, and roll to Pine Tree Circle. Here, you can enjoy healthy sandwiches and salads at the Water Lily Café or a more upscale repast at the Canyon Bistro. Stop at Topanga Homegrown to find a special gift for a friend or go to Hidden Treasures for a vintage second-hand treat at bargain prices. You can't miss bawdy Boubalina's, a fun place to shop for trendy attire.

Topanga Canyon remains an enclave for artistic eccentrics, but is enjoying an uplifting gentrification that includes a massive new library that serves as a focal point for community events. The annual "Artists Tour" in the spring takes you inside the homes of laid-back hipsters as well as the luxurious estates of the landed gentry tucked into the oak woodlands cooled by a sea breeze wafting up the canyon.

Topanga State Park
>www.parks.ca.gov/?page_id=629
>Pine Tree Circle 122 N. Topanga Canyon Blvd.

(6) Hondo Canyon - Hidden Gem

A fairyland of wildflowers accompanied by a choir of birdsong awaits the hiker who enters the Backbone Trailhead on Saddle Peak Road. A downhill cakewalk takes the happy wanderer through stands of majestic woodland oak that shade the seasonal creek in Hondo Canyon. The corridor from Old Topanga Canyon Road to Malibu Canyon, which includes Hondo Canyon, was purchased by the Santa Monica Conservancy for $6 million in the late '80s. Today, it is one of the least-traveled trails in the 450-acre Santa Monica Recreational Area.

The footpath is best enjoyed with a friend and a shuttle of vehicles. Deposit one car on Old Topanga Canyon, then drive across the spine of the mountains on Saddle Peak Road to the trailhead and park a car there, or have a friend drop you off. You will enjoy heart-catching, 360-degree views from this vantage point. Like the corniche overlooking the Côte-d'Azur in the south of France, Saddle Peak Road lets you gaze over the tile roofs of Mediterranean homes clinging to the hillside, with vistas of the ocean shimmering in the distance. The high-rises of the megalopolis of Los Angeles stand tall in the distance like the enchanting Emerald City. To the north, the San Fernando Valley floor stretches to the Los Padres mountains.

Old Topanga Canyon Road, far below, was part of the stagecoach road from Calabasas to the ocean and once linked with the El Camino Real. Highwaymen plagued early travelers, liberating them of their worldly possessions. Floods often washed out the rutted road at Garrapata and Topanga creek intersection, making the road impassable. The Garrapata Bridge, built in 1916, changed all that.

Fire is a fact of life in the Santa Monica mountains. Traces of the fire that burned upper Hondo Canyon in late 1993 remain. It is estimated that fire covered the area 500 times in the 11,500 years since the ice age. What homeowners in the canyons dread is part of the life-giving process that allows re-birth and re-generation in many of the plant species here. The Chumash Indians routinely burned the hills to create fertilizer and to clear brush that blocked the sun to plants they could eat.

Many of the plants in the canyons, like the yellow bush poppy, have seeds that have lain dormant for decades which are released in the growth cycle after a fire. The chaparral slopes—with no recent prior appearance of bush poppy—were covered with thousands of seedling plants in the spring of 1994. The next season, the bush poppies were 4 or 5 feet high, but bloomless. In early March of 2002, a thick blanket of brilliant yellow blooms on stems as tall as trees covered the canyon walls.

17

On the lush shady trail you will see bright orange stands of Indian Paint brush, deep purple wild peony, and sweet peas. I strolled in silence through tree tunnels of sumac and manzanita, shaded by majestic oaks. My trail-mate snagged a few leaves from a bay tree for her spaghetti that night. You should not hike this trail alone. It is not well-maintained. Very few hikers make it to the top of Hondo and there is no cell-service.

We took a rest on the sun-drenched sandstone promontory that juts into the canyon, overlooking a gorge. This is a good place to be still and just listen. An owl who had lost track of time was hooting boldly in the middle of the day. The ubiquitous bushtit—the voice of the chaparral—staked his territory with his call, while the squawk of the bossy scrub jay echoed across the canyon.

Shuttle directions in if you go: Drop one car off on Old Topanga Canyon Road at the Backbone Trailhead just north of the Garrapata Bridge a short distance from the Topanga Canyon post office. Then, shoot back to Topanga Canyon, head toward the beach, and turn right on Fernwood Pacifica. It will turn into Tuna Canyon and then merge with Saddle Peak Road. Drive several miles across the spine of the mountains and, just below the radio tower, you will find parking and the marked trailhead.

The Water Lily in the nearby Pine Tree Circle is a casual stop for a sandwich or salad. Chill and enjoy a cooling breeze coming up the canyon while dining at the outdoor tables.

For a more upscale repast, try the Canyon Bistro where you can enjoy a glass of wine with your meal.

Hondo Canyon

>www.trails.lacounty.gov/Trail/72/backbone-trail---
>hondo-canyon-trail

Canyon Bistro

>www.canyonbistrotopanga.com/

Water Lily Cafe

>www.waterlilycafe.com/
>Pine Tree Circle 122 N. Topanga Canyon Blvd.
>Topanga, Ca. 90290

Mountain Mermaid

>For a very special experience in the canyon stay at the
>Mountain Mermaid. Nature, serenity, and beauty are
>the prime amenities at this bucolic historic retreat.
>http://www.themountainmermaid.com

(7) Fall Splendor In Malibu Creek State Park

In fall, the air is crisp and invigorating, inviting hikers to get outdoors. A soft breeze lifts fat cinnamon leaves from the limbs of sycamore trees. The leaves float gently to earth where they cover the ground in a fecund carpet of burnt orange. Red berries of the toyon shrub brighten the scene of dun-colored grasses bent low over rolling hills. The trail from the entrance off Las Virgenes/Malibu Canyon traces Malibu Creek where ducks dabble for treats and big blue herons stand stalk-still. You can take a short walk to the rock pool where the volcanic rock walls are dark with water seeps, and birds hiding in the reeds sally forth in pursuit of tasty insects. I prefer to walk through the heart of the park on a stretch of the Backbone Trail past Century Lake, a tiny reservoir created in 1901 when the parkland was owned by Crags Country Club. The Forest trailhead just past the second bridge crossing the creek takes you to a cool glen shaded by redwood trees planted by club members. The less-traveled path lined with frilly ferns, and green moss traces Triunfo Creek back to the dam and Century Lake.

If you venture further into the park, you will run into remnants of the M*A*S*H set destroyed by fire. The opening shot of the helicopter flying low over the mountains in the Korean War-era series that went off the air in 1983 was taken here in the back canyon of Malibu Creek Park. The river valley beyond the set, stippled with lemon and orange willows, is a favorite setting for local artists. You can continue on all the way to Bull Dog Motorway that takes you to Castro Peak and circle back to the entrance for an 8-mile loop. The Lookout Trail affords great views of the rocky crags of Goat Buttes and the river corridor.

Easy access to the extended trail network with proximity to suburban tracts makes this a popular park for hikers, mountain bikers, and equestrians. Bring a picnic lunch. You can still find a quiet place to relax in a corner of the favorite park in the heart of the Santa Monica Mountain Conservancy.

Malibu Creek State Park
 www.parks.ca.gov/?page_id=614

Note: Malibu Creek was severely scorched in the 2018 Woolsey Fire, but it is recovering quickly. The trails are open, but the overnight campground is closed. Check with the park site before going for current status.

(8) Urban Oasis - Franklin Canyon

Nestled in a protected canyon midway between Beverly Hills and the San Fernando Valley, you will find shady glens and still waters framed in pines and willows. Although this park is not on the coast, it is one of my favorites. Franklin Canyon Park is a respite from the crush of humanity and the din of city noise, and a wonderful place to give it all a rest. A lovely network of well-groomed trails throughout upper and lower Franklin make it easy for bicyclists and hikers to enjoy a workout in nature without having to drive great distances.

The pond in upper Franklin, with colorful wood ducks nesting in the trees, is fun for toddlers. In winter months, the larger reservoir attracts migrants like buffleheads, scaup and shoveler ducks. Year-round residents include the ubiquitous mud hen and mallards. Turtles bask on the rocks in summer. An osprey is seen upon occasion, sitting high upon a pine bough, waiting to swoop up unsuspecting fish with extended talons.

I am so grateful to have this tranquil oasis so close to friends in Studio City. If I feel like a bun-burner, I hike the 2.3 mile Hastian Trail and rest in the meadow at the end of the that hike. If I have less time, I take the Ranch Trail, beginning at the southwest corner of the reservoir that hugs the canyon wall overlooking a thick forest of eucalyptus and sycamores. This trail, lined with wildflowers, connects with Lake Drive which will take you back to upper Franklin.

Sitting on a bench overlooking the lake, shaded by willows leafing out in spring and cooled by a soft breeze ruffling the waters, I spotted a tri-colored heron. Excited squeals of children spying their first ducks floated on the air. I enjoyed my picnic lunch and savored a couple of peaceful hours in the middle of an otherwise busy day. We are so lucky that conservationist Sooky Goldman, along with Congressman Howard Berman, encouraged the National Park Service to purchase the 605 acres and make them part of the Santa Monica National Recreation Area.

The main entrance to the park is at Mulholland and Coldwater on Franklin Canyon Drive across from Tree People. You can park in the Tree People lot, where plant restoration is in full progress, and hike the more heavily-trafficked Fryman Canyon loop. Joggers and dog-walkers love the ridge trail overlooking the San Fernando Valley. It winds down into Fryman Estates, one of the most prestigious neighborhoods in the valley. It is fun to stroll past the gated mansions sheltered in towering pines with all the amenities the rich and famous feel are required and wonder what it might be like to live there.

There are amphitheaters in both parks where outdoor programs take place. Check their respective sites for scheduled events.

Beware: Heed the photo-enforced STOP signs in the park.

Franklin Canyon Park
   www.mrca.ca.gov/parks/park-listing/franklin-canyon-park/

To learn more about programs and exact directions, go to **LA Mountains**
   www.mrca.ca.gov/

(9) Best Of The Backbone Trail

Enter a shady glade and leave the busy world behind on this little-known trail that just might be the prettiest one left in the Santa Monica mountains. Ninety percent of the national park was blackened in the 2018 Woolsey fire and it will take at least two seasons to bring it back to its natural splendor. The mountains east of Las Virgenes Canyon/Malibu Canyon were spared the devastation of the largest fire in California history.

There is a decision to make when you are about a football-field-length into the walk. Be sure to go to the right through some tall grass that makes it clear this is not a well-traveled track. The trail hugs the canyon wall overlooking the Canejo Valley framed by the Simi Hills. It takes you through tree tunnels of California lilac, black walnut trees, toyon shrubs, and an occasional oak thrown in for good measure. Since the path is almost entirely in the shadow of the mountain, it is cool, damp, and shady, with bright green moss and shaggy ferns lining the walk. The expansive, head-spinning views, uninterrupted by the footprint of mankind, will set your heart racing. It is an undulating march with very little elevation gain and only a few stone stair steps along the way.

You can see the grey peaks stacked in the distance damaged by the fire, a stark reminder of how lucky we are to have this trail intact to enjoy. I was in the process of writing this book and was distressed to see a half-dozen of my favorite outings completely destroyed and closed to the public because of hazardous conditions. The silver lining is that I had to branch out and explore to find replacement trails, and was thrilled to discover this one.

This segment of the Backbone Trail—the trail traverses 69.5 miles from Point Mugu to Will Rogers State Park—extends 3.64 miles and delivers you to Piuma Road in Monte Nido. I did an "in-and-out" and found it enchanting in both directions. What a find! So much wildness so close to civilization. I did encounter a couple of lone humans on the trail, though I would not suggest you hike here solo. The trailhead is on a remote stretch of Stunt Road. Weekend warriors come here on motorcycles and classic cars to the nearby intersection of Stunt and Saddle Peak roads for the views that extend to the Pacific. But beyond that, there are no people to come to your rescue. Details of this hike can be found in *The Complete Hiker's Guide to the Backbone Trail.*

There are no eateries nearby, with the exception of the pricey Saddle Peak Lodge in Monte Nido. So, pull up a rock and enjoy the quietude and the goodies in your backpack on this one. I promise you won't be disappointed.

The Backbone Trail
    www.nps.gov/samo/planyourvisit/backbonetrail.htm

The Complete Hiker's Guide to the Backbone Trail
    www.amazon.com/Complete-Hikers-Guide-
    Backbone-Trail/

(10) King Gillette Ranch - Heart Of The Park

Whenever I enter King Gillette Ranch off Mulholland Highway in Calabasas, I do so with an attitude of gratitude. Stately Spanish colonial revival buildings, manicured lawns, and a man-made water element grace the grounds. An orchard attracts a variety of birds, deer browse the meadows, and 4,000 oak trees populate the slopes, all within easy walking distance of neighboring Malibu Creek State Park.

A quiet battle raged when Soka University decided to sell the 600-acre valley in the heart of the Santa Monica mountains. Developers had been vying for the property, but Soka told the state if they could come up with $35 million, they would sell to them first. It was nip-and-tuck battle for several years. A monumental effort to gather funds to close the deal nearly failed, and this critical part of our park was almost lost. Fortunately for all of us, several agencies pulled together and the funds were raised just in time.

Today, the site is managed harmoniously by the National Park Service, Mountains Recreation & Conservation Authority, Santa Monica Mountains Conservancy, and California State Parks. This makes for an interesting parking situation. You can park for two hours for free at the NP headquarters and check out wonderful interactive displays and visit the gift shop while you are there. If you park inside the grounds there is a $7 fee, but you can stay as long as you like.

The one-mile loop to Inspiration Point takes you through oak woodlands and up to a knoll overlooking the peaks of Malibu Creek State Park. The best view is a 360-degree panorama that proves itself as the *heart of the park*. A spur off the main loop that takes you back to the man-made lake adds a fun dimension to the walk for those who need more exercise. A new "Ridgeline Trail" covering about a three-mile round-trip just opened. It takes the hiker through chaparral, oak woodland, and grasslands. Deer, bobcat, and coyote are just some of the wildlife you can run into here. This outdoor day calls for a picnic by the pond where heron, egrets, ducks, and grebe hang out. Thankfully, it will remain this way for a very long time. There are numerous inviting picnic tables scattered throughout the grounds.

The national park hosts a number of events at their Spanish colonial headquarters. Local artists display their wares on specified days. There are docent-led tours for those interested in the medicinal qualities of the native plants led by a Chumash shaman. Go online to www.samofund.org/calendar for the publication of outdoor events planned at the center. Be sure to stop in the gift shop where local artists' work is on display along with a diorama for the kids.

King Gillette Ranch

www.mrca.ca.gov/parks/park-listing/king-gillette-ranch/

Take Highway 101 (Ventura Freeway) to the Las Virgenes/Malibu Canyon exit. Head south on Las Virgenes Road and continue to Mulholland Highway, about two miles. Turn left onto Mulholland Highway and immediately look for the King Gillette Ranch entrance on the right.

(11) Paradise On A Platter

With rusty anchors and chains, restaurateur Bob Morris has created a nautical setting at Paradise Cove Beach Café that rivals anything I've found in Hawaii for casual beach dining. Relax on a wooden lawn chair on the sun-swept shore with waves crashing at your feet and enjoy a cool one while waiting for a table beneath umbrellas. Inside the café, window seats overlook the sparkling sea. The room is lined with nostalgic black-and-white panoramas of old Malibu. Movies filmed here include *Sea Hunt*, *Beach Blanket Bingo*, and *Gidget*.

Bob Morris's family owned the land at Paradise Cove 35 years ago, but his father, Papa Joe, sold it. In 1996, Morris was able to repurchase the café and parking lot for what is arguably the most idyllic beach in So Cal. Point Dume juts out to the north, forming a scenic protective barrier for the bay. In the summer, it's so calm, young mothers bring tots to get their first taste of the sea. The pier to the south, once used by fishermen to launch their boats, has fallen into disrepair. Pelican, cormorant, and seagulls are all that fish from it today. The historic railway trestle built by May K. Rindge once stretched across Ramirez Canyon just above Paradise Cove. The Queen of Malibu spent most of her fortune waging legal battles to prevent Southern Pacific and road builders from crossing her 17,500 acres of prime coastal land that stretched from Topanga Canyon to the Ventura County Line.

At low tide, you can walk for miles on the most scenic strip of sand in Malibu. Mounds of magenta bougainvillea tumble over chalk-white cliffs lined with mansions. There are sea caves and tide pools to explore on the way to a steep stairwell that takes you to the best whale-watching spot in the "Bu." Follow the wooden boardwalk to the viewing platform overlooking aquamarine waters where sea lions play in wafting kelp forests.

Paradise Cove Beach Café is open for breakfast, lunch, and dinner. The menu ranges from creative omelets and sandwiches to seafood samplers on ice. Four-hour parking is free when you dine at the café and $25 if you don't. There is a changing room, outdoor shower, and clean restrooms for the use of all visitors. It's best to come here in the winter months, making it a fun place to share with holiday guests. In summer, it can be hard to find a place to spread your beach towel.

Paradise Cove
www.paradisecovemalibu.com/

(12) El Matador - Olé!

Want to ditch the crowds and get away from the noise of the city? Do you yearn for a quiet stroll along a lonely seashore, listening to the crush of waves pounding in from a 2000-mile fetch? Just head up Pacific Coast Highway, past Broad Beach Road, to El Matador State Park. A steep stairwell of 150 steps keeps many from enjoying what is one of the last naturally beautiful beaches on our coast. The red bluffs, lined with wind-bent cypress, remind me of Monterey and points north. You can scamper through rock tunnels and caves carved by ceaseless waves, or just sit and watch cormorants and pelicans sitting atop sea stacks. You might spot the head of a seal among the bobbing kelp. Often, dolphin can be seen surfing in the aquamarine waters. You can amble for miles in either direction if you time your visit at low tide.

It is tempting to swim here, but there are no lifeguards in the winter months and only on the weekends in summer. Still, experienced body-boarders ride the waves winter and summer. You need to pack a snack if you plan to spend the day. Happily, there is not one fast food stand in sight. This may be the most photogenic strand of sand on our coast, so don't be surprised if you run into an amateur film shoot. The searing sunsets that crown a day at El Matador are worth waiting for. If you need sustenance, stop at the Vintage Grocers located in the Trancas Country Mart at PCH and Broad Beach Road and get a box lunch to go.

Don't tell anyone, but if you take Broad Beach Road off of Pacific Coast Highway at Trancas to the left up to Bunny Lane you will find access to the coast. The entrance to La Chuza beach is an inviting "Alice in Wonderland" tunnel past estates on a bluff overlooking the sea that leads down about 100 steep steps to the shore. Young lovers spread beach towels here in the alcoves scalloped in chalk-white cliffs. If you come at low tide, you can walk through sea caves to El Matador. Go at sunset and get a spectacular show. Swim at your peril as there are no lifeguards.

El Matador State Beach—32215 Pacific Coast Highway, Malibu. It's easy to miss the small brown sign pointing to the parking lot between Broach Beach and Decker Canyons.

Download a free tide chart app from Google Play so you know the best time to go.

El Matador State Beach
    www.parks.ca.gov/?page_id=633
Lechuza
    www.californiabeaches.com/beach/lechuza-beach/
Vintage Grocery—Trancas Country Market, 30745 Pacific Coast Highway.

(13) Sandstone Peak - Inspiration Point

The fastest way to lose the crowds in L.A. is to drive up Pacific Coast Highway past the Ventura County line. About a half-hour drive north of Santa Monica, make a hard right turn onto Yerba Buena and head for the heavens. This less-traveled road snakes 6.5 miles up the rim of Sycamore Canyon, through pasturelands sheltered from the blustery coastal winds, to the Mishe Mokwa trailhead parking lot. Stop on the way at the Circle X cabin to register your intentions to hike in the park with the rangers and pick up a map.

The six-mile Sandstone Peak loop offers a mixed sampler of early California plant communities, and takes you to the highest point in the Santa Monica Mountain Conservancy. It's worth a bit of extra effort to take the steep steps up to the monument at the top of 3,111-foot Sandstone Peak. The carrot on the end of the stick is an eye-popping view from Inspiration Point of the coastline from Santa Barbara to the Pacific Palisades peninsula.

The trail takes you through Carlyle Canyon where rock climbers test their mettle on the sheer walls of Echo Cliff. A house-sized boulder delicately balanced on a small rock beneath a giant split rock conjures images of the Southwest. Giant sandstone formations and jaw-dropping views from Inspiration Point make this six-mile loop a favorite for hikers.

It is easy to imagine the native Chumash people living happily here in days gone by. Traces of their village in nearby Leo Carrillo Beach far below date them back about 7,000 years. They came into these foothills to gather acorns and black walnuts, and to hunt game. They pounded the acorns from the oak trees to a fine powder in rock mortars. From the acorn base, they created a bland paste, much like the Hawaiian poi, that was the staple of their diet. If you are yearning for something more flavorful after your hike, it is a straight shot down the face of the mountain on Yerba Buena to Neptune's Net on PCH. Celebrities from Malibu, bikers, surfers, hikers, and seafood nuts haunt this funky beach café year-round.

Note: This hike is a cornerstone of the national park system. It remains closed at the time of this writing because of damage done by the Woolsey fire. However, Neptune's Net has re-opened and I believe this trail will be repaired sooner than most. Check with the site before going. It is a bit a drive and I don't want you to be disappointed.

Sandstone Peak loop entrance at Mishe-Mokwa Trailhead
    www.alltrails.com/trail/us/california/mishe-mokwa-trail-to-sandstone-peak-trail

Park Headquarters at the Circle X Ranch
    www.nps.gov/samo/planyourvisit/circlexranch.htm

Neptune's Net
    www.neptunesnet.com/

(14) Ray Miller Trail - Where Backbone Trail Begins

Plaque at trailhead for Ray Miller: Guardian of the Canyon 1902 to 1989

Ray Miller trailhead marks the beginning of the 69.12 mile · Backbone Trail that takes the hiker across the spine of the Santa Monica mountains, through oak forests, shady glens, and rock gardens, all the way to Will Rogers State Park on

Sunset Boulevard. A few hardy souls hike the entire length of the trail in one exhausting week, camping out along the way each year. I chose to do segments of the trail at my leisure. In their book, *The BackBone Trail*, Doug and Caroline Chamberlin have taken the guesswork out of the trail that has evolved over the last 40 years into one contiguous hike. Portions of the track are owned by several different bureaucratic entities so the rules of the road are different in various segments of the trail. Their comprehensive book on the Backbone Trail network should be required reading for anyone hiking in the Santa Monica mountains.

However, Ray was the first to claim this trail. He came to the sunny coastal clime to get out of the cold country when he was 72. He lived in the Pt. Mugu State Park and slept in his rusted-out Volkswagen. For ten years, he greeted guests at the trailhead, letting them know about washouts and other possible dangers. He took note of whoever entered the park that day and made certain that they got out that night. This was an unofficial task that he took upon himself. For many years, he was considered a vagrant by the park officials. One day, the rangers routed him out of the park, but, instead of arresting him as he'd expected, they'd measured him for a uniform. The Backbone Trailhead is named after him, and he was given an award for the highest number of volunteer hours ever to be given to the Park Service.

The day I entered the trail, I heard a canyon wren trilling sweetly. As I hiked steadily upward, a mountain quail warned her flock of fledglings with a crisp, "Chicago," that I was intruding upon their world. A young buck with velvet knobs on his head stood on the knoll to the left, watching me go by. Dead ahead, the Pacific lay shrouded in a gauzy marine layer floating up the cleft of the canyon that I had to myself.

This is one of the many trails carved into the canyons by the Chumash Indians that has been in use for about 7,000 years. I tried to imagine carrying a heavy load, balanced neatly on the top of my head in a basket, up the steep incline that affords stunning views of the azure Pacific. The Indians used this trail to make inland migrations to the 600-acre expanse of grassland on the summit. They collected materials there to build domed huts called "ops" and to make their wondrous baskets.

The wildflower meadow in the shadow of Bony Ridge with stands of native needle grass is much the same as it was before the arrival of the Spanish in 1542. The trail system connects to Rancho Sierra Vista or Satwiwa, the Indian Cultural Center in Newbury Park. Tribes of native Indians congregated at Satwiwa each year to plan their hunting and ceremonial calendars. Purification services were held in which the medicine man would burn the silver sage, using the smoke to cleanse the soul of the wayward.

You can march along this track to your heart's content. It connects with the La Jolla Canyon Trail that wanders through a back-country meadow. Unfortunately, the La Jolla trailhead off of Pacific Coast Highway was washed out in the rains of 2016, making it impossible to do what was one of the most beautiful loops in the mountains. You can still dip down into Sycamore Canyon with towering trees lining a seasonal streambed. But, beware of bicyclists racing down this track from Rancho Sierra Vista to the coast. Of course, you can remain on the main track which stretches across the entire backbone of the Santa Monica mountains.

Note: Even though the Ray Miller Trail was blackened in the Woolsey fire, I am leaving it in the book because it is the beginning of the Backbone Trail. It is also historically significant as the Chumash Indians used this trail as a trade route to the interior. Segments of the Backbone Trail east of

Las Virgenes/Malibu Canyon are still open and not affected by the fires. You can find those segments detailed in the Chamberlins' book and I have shared two of them here in my book.

Ray Miller Trailhead
www.californiacoastaltrail.info/cms/archives/hike_fav.php?aid=158

The Backbone Trail
www.nps.gov/samo/planyourvisit/backbonetrail.htm

(15) Satwiwa - Rancho Sierra Vista,
"Keeping The Chumash Spirit Alive"

When humans could speak with animals and the world was "safe and warm," the Chumash Indians came up Big Sycamore Canyon, carrying bounty from the sea to trade with the Indians that lived at Satwiwa, a.k.a. Rancho Sierra Vista. Once a year, the tribes of Gabrielino, Tongva, and Chumash would meet in the vast meadow at the top of the 8-mile climb to discuss the hunting and ceremonial plans of the year. Today, the meadow, framed by Boney Ridge, a volcanic bluff that shelters the canyon, is honeycombed with hiking trails.

Take the paved road, a multiuse trail used by cyclist and equestrians, deep into Sycamore Canyon. Make a hard left when you reach the canyon floor and head up the trail tracing a seasonal creek. Shaded by black walnut and sycamore, the path winds through tunnels of California lilac laced with the curly tentacles of wild cucumber. Your only company will be the chatter of the creek, the knock of the acorn woodpeckers, and the lilting song of the thrasher. While you absorb the stillness, imagine a Chumash maiden, carrying dried fish and carved shells in her intricately woven basket, sharing the trail with you. The Chumash, who have lived in the area for 7,000 years, are often listed as extinct, but there are about 2,000 Chumash descendants alive today. Chief Charlie Cook gives talks at Satwiwa, home of the Native Cultural Center, in hopes of keeping the Chumash spirit alive.

You can take Lynn Road off the 101 to the main entrance on Potrero Road, but the prettier way to go is through Hidden Valley to a parking lot on Potrero, which is the backdoor of the park. Take Westlake Blvd (Highway 23) south to Potrero Rd, turn right, and enjoy a Sunday drive through equestrian estates. You will see cars lined up at the trailhead on Potrero. Return on this same route to Westlake.

A great stop for outdoor dining is the Stonehaus Winery and Restaurant on Agoura Road in Westlake.

Trail maps available at the nature center and at:

National Park Service Rancho Sierra Vista/Satwiwa
    www.nps.gov/samo/planyourvisit/rsvsatwiwa.htm

Stonehaus Restaurant and winery
    www.nps.gov/samo/planyourvisit/rsvsatwiwa.htm

(16) Buena Ventura - Land Of Good Fortune

The wonderful thing about the historic district in Ventura is that it is a walking town. The mountains, the sea, the vintage shops, and eateries are all within easy reach from free all-day parking lots on California Street. Remnants of the classic California beach town cars are not zooming by; they are cruising and politely stopping for pedestrians browsing shops while enjoying the sea breeze and sunshine. Shady gardens, especially the courtyard at the San Buena Ventura Mission, invite the visitor to sit a spell, while bells ringing from City Hall chime out, "I Did it My Way."

The folks in Ventura love the outdoors and have created a fabulous botanical garden that begins just behind City Hall at the top of California Street. It snakes up a canyon, switch-backing through rock gardens planted with succulents and cactus found in Mediterranean climes about

43

the globe. It is an easy climb to flower-festooned meadows and vistas that extend from Boney Ridge overlooking Camarillo to the south and to the Channel Islands sitting prominently on the horizon. I met the "Social Climbers," a band of retired teachers, many young women with a babies strapped to their chests, and a host of mutts on leashes followed by proud owners. You are advised to come early as there is little shade and it is a popular track.

On Main Street, a block below City Hall, you will find a number of hiker-friendly restaurants. I liked the Saloon BBQ for its tri-tip salad. Just below Main on California Street, the Lure, an upscale fish house, offers wonderfully fresh seafood. After lunch, I suggest you saunter down California Street to the ocean for a stroll along the boardwalk, tracing the waterfront to Surfer's Point where windsurfers fill the sky like colorful confetti. Sadly, the famous Ventura Pier is closed due to damage in El Nino, and the high surf has piled rocks along the shore, but you can still walk the eight miles of the San Buena Ventura Beach. Cap your day off with a cool one at the Crown Plaza Hotel open-air beach bar.

Exit 101 on California Street. Parking is free all day at numerous lots on California Street.

Stop at the **Ventura Visitors Bureau**, 101 South California Street, for helpful maps and more day-trip suggestions
    visitventuraca.com/visit/visitors-center/

V entura Botanical Gardens
    www.venturabotanicalgardens.com/

Note: The botanical garden was in the path of the Thomas Fire in Dec. 2017. The 109-acre garden was severely damaged and closed for over a year. Major repairs were made and the park was re-opened to the public in Dec. 2018.

(17) Carpinteria - Bluff Walk And Baby Cake Beach

When the inland valleys are sizzling, I shoot up the coast to Carpinteria to "chillax" for a day or two. The scent of the sea and laid-back lifestyle evocative of early California are worth the drive. First stop is at the Carpinteria Bluffs Nature Preserve where you can stroll through the meadow spiked with silver sage overlooking the Santa Barbara Channel to the railroad tracks. Bear to your right and discover one of four onshore seal rookeries left in California. Peer over Sidenberg Overlook to see newborn harbor seals frolic while their moms snooze on the sand. Turn around and take the walk down to a lonely stretch of beach with fun tide-pooling and a host of shorebirds, including great blue heron, egrets, and pelicans that swoop low on patrol for snacks. The path descending to the beach is a bit dodgy, but you can do it. This stroll beneath the bluffs is one of the prettiest wild walks left on the California coast.

For more than two decades, a battle raged between development interests with plans to build huge housing and hotel projects and local conservationists who wanted to preserve the bluffs. Surfers, hikers, and birdwatchers have long enjoyed the bluffs, which rise about 100 feet above the beach, offering great views of Anacapa, Santa Cruz, and Santa Rosa islands. In 1998, the Carpinteria Bluffs were declared a nature center to be preserved for all to enjoy.

When hunger calls, take Carpinteria Drive north to Linden Avenue and check out one of the many eateries springing up in this sweet coastal town. Stop for a cool one at the sweatband-friendly outdoor patio at Cabo's Baja Grill or try the Cajun Kitchen, a local favorite for lunch or breakfast. The Siam Elephant is a wonderful Tai Restaurant with delicious food at reasonable prices and covered outdoor seating.

Linden Avenue dead-ends at Carpinteria Beach where the baby cake surf is safe enough for toddlers. Don't forget your boogie board to ride long, rolling waves. This beach was once the site of a large Chumash settlement. The tar that wells up on the south end of the white sand shoreline provided a waterproof material used to seal their seaworthy vessels called "tomols." Today, there are 250 choice campsites nestled in trees along the shore that accommodate RVs, trailers or tents.

Don't miss the birding opportunity at the salt marsh sanctuary on the north end of the beach. A multitude of song birds flit among the indigenous gardens lacing the tide channels. Shorebirds, buffleheads, and ruddy ducks are found here, along with the ubiquitous coot, or mud hen. This is one of the few salt marshes remaining in Southern California. The reeds and shrubs in the marsh must transform the salt and endure two influxes of tide daily. There are self-guiding plaques throughout the preserve. Docents lead tours every Saturday at 10AM throughout the year.

Directions: Exit 101 onto 150 and cross over to Carpinteria Drive, turn right to the parking lot at Carpinteria Bluffs. After your walk, return to the surface street. Take it to Linden which is lined with shops and eateries.

City of Carpinteria Official site
www.carpinteria.ca.us/

Carpinteria Bluffs
www.californiabeaches.com/beach/carpinteria-bluffs-nature-preserve/

(18) Arroyo Burro- Sweet Spot In Santa Barbara

Arroyo Burro Beach, a wide strip of powdery sand locals call Hendry's, is my favorite stop in Santa Barbara. The trailhead at the southern tip of the parking lot leads to More Mesa, a bluff walk with stunning views of the coast. Parasailers glide overhead beneath flashy canopies, pelicans patrol the bluffs in v-shaped formations, while, far below, the aquamarine Pacific purls into billows of foaming white. Irish-green grass dotted with wildflowers carpets the mesa that is shaded by giant sycamores in the spring. You will likely have this walk to yourself save the occasional local walking dogs often off-leash. Continue out of the park onto Medcliff Road to Mesa Lane and turn right to the Mesa steps. Take the public stairwell down to the seashore. Enjoy a contemplative stroll on this stretch of hard-packed sand backed by craggy cliffs back to the Arroyo Burro parking lot and facilities. Be sure you are not walking this stretch at high tide before embarking.

After this two-mile loop, you will be ready for lunch at the Boat House that rests on the sand overlooking the beach. Zesty seafood pasta was my choice, but shrimp Louis salad and lobster rolls are also on the menu, among many other delicious choices. Diners can enjoy the patio shielded from the wind by glass barriers, or dine inside in casual elegance. Happy Hour offers tasty treats at bargain prices. There is a hamburger stand next to the restaurant for folks in a hurry. A snooze on the sand after a sumptuous repast is in order.

The ocean is relatively calm here and safe to swim. You can walk for miles up the long strand of sand beneath the cliffs. Locals with blankets and lawn chairs gather here to watch the sun slip into the Pacific in a fiery crescendo to cap off a perfect Santa Barbara day.

Arroyo Burro Beach County Park is located 5 miles west of Santa Barbara's city center on Cliff Drive near Hope Ranch. From Highway 101, take Las Positas Road south to Cliff Drive. Turn right and travel 1/2 mile to the park entrance.

Arroyo Burro Beach Park
> www.countyofsb.org/parks/day-use/arroyo-burro-beach.sbc

Boat House Restaurant
> www.boathousesb.com/

(19) Santa Cruz Island In The Channel Islands National Park

Power-packed outdoor days restore the soul, rejuvenate the body, and clear the mind.

About an hour north of Los Angeles, a spectacular day trip to the island of Santa Cruz awaits you. Turn up at the Island Packer dock in Ventura Harbor about 9 AM with a lunch in your backpack and leave your worries behind. After an hour-long cruise across the channel, passengers are dropped off at Scorpion Anchorage and admonished to be back by 4 PM or to plan on spending the night on the island. Some choose to do exactly that, but most fan out on separate day hikes.

Santa Cruz, the largest of all the Channel Islands, offers the most varied hiking and opportunity for self-exploration. The stiff hike up to Cavern Point overlooking Scorpion Anchorage takes you to the shadeless North Bluff Trail. This easy march traces the bluffs and calls for binoculars for spotting birds in the meadow and marine life in the vast expanse of blue spread out before you. Far below, kelp forests sway in aquamarine waters where golden Garibaldi fish and sea lions play. The trail ends at the turquoise horseshoe bay called Potato Harbor that is a perfect spot for your picnic.

No humans, save national park rangers, live on the island today. But for thousands of years, this was the domain of the Chumash Indians. Legend has it that the "people" sprouted here from seeds and became so numerous that Hutash, the earth god, created a rainbow bridge for them to go to the mainland. While crossing, many of the people tumbled into the sea and became playful dolphins. It is tempting to believe that the pod of 1,500 dolphin that leap madly about the Island Packer boat on this journey are enlivened by the spirits of the people. Gray whales migrating through the channel on the way to and from their breeding grounds in Baja are often seen on the crossing to the mainland. The skipper often takes time to follow them, even if you are not on a whale-watch cruise.

51

Wrap up this day with the seafood sampler at Brophy Brothers' upstairs glass-enclosed patio overlooking the yachts tied up in Ventura Harbor. The best viewing of the sunset is on the beach on the other side of the harbor parking lot. The surf is a bit rough for swimming, but you can take a nice long stroll on a less-traveled stretch of sand to the south where you will meet lots of shorebirds.

There is much more to learn about the Channel Islands National Park and the Island Packer offerings on their website. Be sure to make reservations in advance.

Channel Islands National Park
   www.nps.gov/chis/index.htm

Brophy Brothers
   www.brophybros.com/welcome-ventura/

(20) Lake Cachuma - Godda Bless

If you sneeze, you will miss the entrance to Lake Cachuma Recreation Area midway between Santa Barbara and Los Olivos on Highway 154. The sparkling man-made lake flanked by the Santa Ynez and San Rafael mountains fills a valley that was once a sacred meeting place for the Chumash people. Resting in the Pacific Flyway, it is a winter home to thousands of migrant birds. You can take the 2-hour eagle cruise on the open-air pontoon boat with a naturalist guide to point out the wildlife along the shore and share the cultural riches of the area. You will spot bald and golden eagle, osprey, Canadian geese, western grebes and a variety of ducks. Deer are often seen standing on their hind legs munching on the lichen they consider a delicacy that hangs from the limbs of oak trees along the shore.

Gliding through sheltered coves reveals California as it was thousands of years ago. Chumash gathered in this valley during the winter solstice for celebrations. Many tribes congregated here for feasting, games, and ceremonial fun. California Golden Eagle—Slo'w (Chief of the First People) was a prominent figure in Chumash culture. He was considered chief of all animals. The giant chief of the sky supported the upper world on his wings; his movements caused the phases of the moon and eclipse. Here in the "Middle World," eagle feathers were often used for ceremonial dance regalia.

After your cruise, enjoy a picnic lunch (bring your own; there are no food concessions) at one of the many tables resting in the shade of stately oaks. Then take one of the self-guided hikes. The undulating Sweetwater Trail that begins in Harvey Cove traces the lake's edge. The shady amble lets you breathe deeply of the sage-scented chaparral and offers more good birding ops and a chance for solitude.

A variety of boats are for rent year-round at the Rocky Mountain Recreation Company for those who want to cruise on their own. Lake Cachuma is 18 miles from Santa Barbara at 2225 Highway 154. There is small fee at the gate and plenty of parking for hikers and campsites. You can even rent a yurt. Make reservations for the eagle or wildlife cruise in advance at 1-805-686-5055.

A fun stop on the way back to Santa Barbara is the Cold Streams Tavern, the famous stagecoach stop in San Marcos Pass. On the weekends, they have live music and casual outdoor dining. Hearty traditional meals are served inside the rustic lodge.

You will find cruise times and information about boat rentals and camping facilities here:

Cachuma Lake Recreation
www.countyofsb.org/parks/parks05.aspx?id=13440

Cold Streams Tavern
www.coldspringtavern.com/

(21) Parma Park - Santa Barbara

If you are in the mood for solitude and head-spinning views, I have the hike for you. This little-known, less-traveled trail system spanning 200 acres is the largest urban park in Santa Barbara. You might run into a few locals with dogs on leash or see a couple parasailers gliding overhead, but you will likely have the 5-mile trail system to yourself.

This trailhead is easy to reach. Just take Highway 144, also known as Sycamore Canyon, to Highway 192. This will take you on a scenic drive through lush, wooded foothills of Santa Barbara. When 192 becomes Starwood Drive, start looking for trailhead markers. There are six entrances to Parma Park. I entered where there is a miniscule sign indicating the trailhead called Starwood East on maps of the area. The main entrance is about a half-mile north. The trail is a loop, so whether you lean to the left or go to the right, you will find yourself climbing up switchbacks to incredible vistas. In the distance, the purple mountains of the Channel Islands rest on the blue horizon, framed in a fringe of swaying palms on the coast at Butterfly Beach.

I visited Parma Park over the Christmas holiday when the temps are cool and perfect for hiking. I was shocked when I attempted to hike nearby Inspiration Point listed in all of the hiking books. Cars were parked for miles on Tunnels Road and throngs of hikers were heading to the famous waterfalls that were, no doubt, dry from the five-year drought in Southern California. The popular Cold Creek Canyon and San Ysidro trailheads are closed due to the horrific mudslides in Montecito. Trails that remain open are heavily-trafficked. Parma is a wonderful respite and a good workout for those who like a little burn with the reward of forever views.

While you are in the neighborhood, why not continue on 192 to Mission Canyon Road, turn right, and take in the Santa Barbara Botanic Garden? It is a civilized walk through creations made of indigenous plants and succulents that love the Mediterranean climate. Do the loop that takes in a shady redwood forest and enjoy cool glades after your hike on Parma which is a shadeless track. If your timing is right, you can partake in a cleansing tea ceremony at the Japanese Tea House.

Parma Park
> www.santabarbaraca.gov/gov/depts/parksrec/parks/features/pathstrails/parma.asp

Santa Barbara Botanic Garden
> www.sbbg.org/explore-garden/garden-sections-displays

(22) Montecito's Hidden Gem

The folks who live in Montecito maintain a trail system that meanders through the backyards of their mansions. I could not find a map for this trail system anywhere. Maybe that is the way the locals want it. Quite by chance, I saw a sign that said, "Trail," on Sheffield Drive and Creekside road just south of the Romano Creek Bridge. I parked by the side of the road, making sure to stay inside the white lines. If you miss this mark, don't despair. There are many trail signs along Sheffield, but you have to keep a sharp eye peeled to spot them,

Yes, much of Montecito was damaged in the horrendous mudslides in 2017, but this section of this gorgeous area remains intact. The unheralded public track winds through creek beds into the tree-tunnels that lead up to vistas enjoyed by the landed gentry. See why Oprah, arguably one of the richest women in the world, calls these hills, sheathed in pines and eucalyptus, home. It is a delightful stroll that feels like following the witch's breadcrumbs to the gingerbread house as you follow the many trail signs along the way. This is a sweet walk with nary a soul to tell you that you are trespassing on private property, or a Doberman pincer charging down the hill to protect his master's estate.

Sadly, Cold Creek Canyon, which was one of Santa Barbara's most popular hikes, is still closed, and Highway 192 that curves around the base of the foothills to the San Ysidro trail is also closed. Crews are still working feverishly to repair the infrastructure destroyed in the mudslides that followed in the wake of the Thomas Fire. I was pleased to find this leg-stretcher nestled between Summerland and Montecito with easy access from the 101 freeway.

After your explorations, roll on over to the village of Montecito on the Village Coast Road. There you will find eateries from casual to elegant. The homemade chile rellenos at Los Arroyos are the best north of the border. Locals favor the Pharmacy in Montecito's upper village, located at the intersection of East Valley and San Ysidro roads, where no one will spot them in their sweats taking a breather from fame and fortune. You can enjoy breakfast or lunch indoors or on the outside patio.

Wherever you land in this enchanted region blessed with sunny skies, a tangy sea breeze, and an abundance of magenta bougainvillea cascading over white walls, it's all good!

Montecito Pharmacy and Cafe
      www. montecitocoffeeshop.com/

Los Arroyos
      www. losarroyos.net/#home-section

(23) Montaña de Oro - Hidden Gem On The Central Coast

Montaña de Oro, mountain of gold, has to be one of the most beautiful bluff walks in the world. Aquamarine swells with immense power ceaselessly pound on the cliffs, forming alcoves with fantastic layered and jagged rock formations that look like stacks of striated pancakes. Tawny, buff-colored cliffs ring the shore. The meadow walk to the cliffs is best seen in the spring, but there are sticky monkey mounds of yellow sage and some small poppies popping in summer. The crisp breath off the churning sea keeps the many hikers coming to Schooner Cove year-round. I saw hundreds of guillemots with black-and-white bomber patches and red feet, a couple of oyster catchers, along with a California quail sitting tall in the meadow. It is a wide, easy march with smaller paths lining steep cliffs and dramatic coves with sandy beaches. The ocean is more energetic and dramatic here than my beaches in Malibu, but too cold to swim in. Still, you can take a snooze on the sand after your hike and enjoy a picnic lunch.

Pick up lunch on the way at the quaint little bedroom community of Baywood. The Back Bay Café overlooking the marina is where locals congregate with canine friends in tow. You can join them for the morning ritual of sharing gossip over a cup of steaming Joe, or pick up a sandwich to go.

If you want to skirt the crowds on the two-mile beach trail, take the Coon Creek Trail. The tree-shaded trail, laced with cucumber vines and wildflowers, traces the course of a trickling stream. It is an easy march into this lush fairyland of cool ferns and mosses. I enjoyed a solitary stroll up the deep canyon. Complete trail maps are available at the park headquarters, located in the original Spooner Ranch house under a lone stand of wind-bent cypress, overlooking Spooner Cove. Overnight campsites are available.

After my hike, I stopped near the park headquarters where lazy Coon Creek enters the sea. There is a sandy beach where you are welcome to stop and take a rest after your walk on the bluffs. Remains discovered here tell us that the Chumash Indians called this cove home as long as 9,000 years ago. I shared the beach with a family of killdeer. The mother did her broken wing trick to lead me away from her two chicks. I am pleased that this place is being preserved not just for the enjoyment of humans, but for all marine and bird life as well.

Directions are simple: Exist 101 at Los Osos Canyon Road and take it all the way to Schooner Cove. I'm taking you a bit further afield in this outdoor day (a 3-hour drive, north of Los Angeles), but, trust me, it is worth it! The park is six miles southwest of Morro Bay and seven miles south of Los Osos on Pecho Road.

At the very end of the road is the entrance to Point Buchon trail which is on private land and is only open to the public from Thursday to Sunday. There is a separate chapter on the Point Buchon Trail.

Montana de Oro
www.parks.ca.gov/?page_id=592

Back Bay Café
www.thebackbaycafe.com/locations/
1399 2nd Street, Baywood Park, CA 93402

(24) Morro Bay - Birding On The Central Coast

Across from the boardwalk that lines Morro Bay estuary, the surf's roar is muffled by white sand dunes wearing a cape of billowing grasses. A cool wind tickled the waters of the Back Bay as I sat on a wooden bench beneath a sprawling cypress while awaiting my kayak guide. The iconic, 576-foot volcanic Morro Rock dwarfs all else in the landscape. January is the time of year when thousands of migrating birds make a stop here on the Pacific Flyway. Ominous clouds were gathering overhead. Showers this time of year are sporadic and usually light. The moan of a lonesome buoy broke the silence of the gray hovering over the bay.

I met Virginia at the Back Bay Marina in the morning before typical afternoon winds picked up. "Leave the paddling to me. Just relax and get your binoculars out," she instructed as I slipped into our two-man kayak.

Virginia loves to take birders out. It gives her great pleasure to get out on the bay and spot her old friends. We paddled in the Back Bay for about a mile before turning into a channel in the estuary where thousands of birds lay waiting. A low-flying flock of double-crested cormorant glided past us in close formation. Tiny-eared grebes among hundreds of buffleheads curled under as we slid by them. Flocks of sanderlings, spotted sandpipers, willet, curlew, and marbled godwit lined the muddy shore of the channel exposed at low tide. They were all busy poking for tidbits. The nutrients in this gooey brown stuff are so rich it has been compared to rain forests for birds.

We were greeted at the mouth of the channel by a colony of harbor seals that haul themselves out on this same bank every day. They fanned their tails to create circulation and keep warm while taking their siesta. Heads with curious charcoal eyes poked up and a performance of playful spirals seemed specifically orchestrated for our pleasure. I felt I was seated in the postcard scenery by green mountains floating on the horizon. This is absolutely the best way to see the birds and marine life in Morro Bay. From the shore, even with extra-strength binoculars, you just can't see the birds clearly. When the tide is high, the kayak rides high enough that you can see even more birds that are tucked away in the brown tussocks of reeds.

During Martin Luther King weekend, the Audubon Society hosts a birding fest in Morro Bay. For a mere $65.00, you can enjoy over 140 events that take you to local birding hotspots as far south as Pismo Beach and as far north as Ragged Point on the Big Sur Coast. A complete list (and directions) to these birding destinations are listed on the

Audubon site, so you can partake in great birding any time of year on your own. There are events for every level of interest—from wide-eyed birder checking off his life list to casual observer adding a new dimension to nature walks.

Competition for the best seafood on the Embarcadero in Morro Bay proper—overlooking fishing boats and yachts in the harbor—is intense. The Blue Sky Café, a local favorite, offers the best Seafood Louie in town. Pan-seared scallops at the Galley got a 5-star review from this hungry birder. Not be outdone, Dorn's, a landmark in the area, signature scampi should not be missed. A stroll on the Embarcadero will garner sightings of sea lions, harbor seals, and sea otters with fluffy kits riding on their mothers' bellies. Upstairs in the nature center, local artists have formed a co-op to share their wares at competitive prices.

The Inn at Morro Bay is nestled at the base of Black Mountain between the Natural History Museum and the heron rookery. It overlooks the bay and sand spit that protects it from the crashing ocean surf. It is an ideal location for explorations in the estuary and surrounds. I looked forward to returning to my cozy room with its fireplace and balcony, perfect for sipping wine and watching the sun slip behind the dunes after a day of exploration.

Morro Bay State Park
> www.parks.ca.gov/?page_id=594

Kayaking in the Central Coast
> www.centralcoastoutdoors.com/kayaking-morro-bay-california/

(25) Whale Trail On The Central Coast

When whales burst from the sea with joyful exaltation, they humble us with their awesome power. Making the longest migrations of any mammal on earth, from Alaska's chilly waters to Baja, California's warmth, they rely on ancient knowledge to guide them. Today, their challenges are greater than ever from congested, noisy shipping lanes, to pollutants and plastic in our oceans. The creation of the Whale Trail, with over sixty designated viewing sites on the Pacific Coast from British Columbia to California, is an attempt to bring greater sensitivity to the survival needs of the largest and oldest creatures on our planet.

Six viewing sites have been identified on the Central Coast of California: San Simeon, Moonstone Beach in Cambria, the pier at Cayucos, the bluff trail in Montaña de Oro State Park, the Avila Pier, and at the Oceano Dunes Overlook at

Grand Avenue. At each site are placards displaying marine mammals people should expect to see from that vantage point and signs to help spot them. Whales are just a part of the marine life that needs our protection.

Shorebirds circling indicate a shoal of fish that will soon bring seals, sea lions, and other sea creatures to the surface. Spouts, or blows, of whales exhaling above the water's surface, often look like puffs of smoke. The shape and size of the blow is distinctive to each species. Gray whales coming through December to April have a double blow-hole with a heart-shaped spout. Humpbacks that can be seen all year long have tall, column-shaped blows. All cetaceans have identifying dorsal fins. Find more information on how to spot and identify marine mammals on TheWhaleTrail.org

I visited the Piedras Lighthouse in San Simeon that sits on a lonely peninsula where rough seas crash over sea stacks. Docents lead tours through the manicured grounds, garnering good viewing spots for a variety of marine life, including the whales during migrations. A fluffy otter was floating on his back, oblivious to crashing waves, while elephant seals lay sprawled on the shore.

The pier in San Simeon Bay on the Whale Trail is the home of the Coastal Discovery Center. Docents love to take kids to the end of the pier where they drop a line into the water to collect a sample, then place it under a microscope for the kids to marvel at the squiggling life forms in a single drop. This is an effort to encourage stewardship of our precious oceans and the creatures who live in them. Locals want to show off their gorgeous region, and they enjoy sharing the trails and their knowledge of flora and fauna at no charge, while they are encouraging *stewardship travel*. You can pick up a Stewardship Traveler Clean-Up Kit and appreciation tote bags at the Avila Beach, Cayucos, and Cambria Visitor Centers.

My favorite stop on the Whale Trail is the pier at Cayucos. It is a fun walk to tide pools as well as an opportunity to see migrating whales and playful sea otters, and it is home to Schooners Restaurant. Savoring an oysters Rockefeller starter, followed by saucy seafood pasta paired with a crisp chardonnay and a front row seat for the sunset is the perfect end to a day exploring the Whale Trail on the Central Coast.

Highway 1 Discovery Route
> www. highway1discoveryroute.com/

Whale Trail
> www. thewhaletrail.org/

Schooners Restaurant
> www.schoonerswharf.com/

(26) Point Buchon - Central Coast

"Go placidly amid the noise and the haste, and remember what peace there may be in silence."

~Max Ehrmann-Desiderata

The Point Buchon trailhead is at the end of Pecho Valley Road that goes through Montaña de Oro State Park. The land is privately owned by a utility company, but it is open to the public on select days. A friendly host greets you and requests that you sign in to ensure that all guests are accounted for at the end of the day. I arrived at about 9 AM to one of the last pristine bluff walks remaining on the Central Coast. It soothed my city-weary soul to be in the still, and to fill my lungs with tangy sea air.

One other hiker, who wanted to mind his own business, shared this lonely stretch of coast with me. I strolled the sea cliffs, overlooking aquamarine waters with dark patches of kelp in the gauzy veil of fog that hugs the Central Coast in blessed silence. The floating forests are home to abundant marine life that includes sea otters and harbor seals that haul themselves up to take a snooze in the sheltered coves. Guillemot and oyster catchers with bright red feet vie for space on sea stacks that are coated white with guano. On a clear day, if you hike up to Windy Point, you will be able to see Diablo, a rather ominous-looking nuclear facility to the south. The round trip is about 6.6 miles round trip if you hike the entire trail.

What you see above the water line is impressive enough, but what is happening below is the true beauty of this place. The waters off Point Buchon have been declared a marine conservation area by the state. Because the tide pools are protected from trampling and collection by humans, the rocky shores shelter plentiful populations of intertidal fish, algae, and invertebrates. The reef harbors an incredible amount of marine diversity, and is known for cold water corals found in unusually shallow water. Of course, you can't observe this from the bluffs that are roped to discourage trespassers, but it is heartening to know that the sea life is thriving here.

The area around the Point Buchon Trail was occupied by Native Americans for over 10,000 years. The magnificent headland known as Point Buchon is named in honor of a prominent Northern Chumash leader so-named Buchon by the Spanish in 1769.

Check with the website to make sure the trail will be open on days that fit your schedule. There is an ample parking lot with facilities and a sign that says, "Private Property," open to hikers Thursday through Sunday.

Point Buchon
    www. bit.ly/2zOBbAk

(27) Point Lobos - Whalers Cove

If there is a prettier walk than the North Shore Trail out of Whalers Cove in Point Lobos, I can't imagine where it is. Windblown cypress shade the rocky path that hugs coves splashed with deep aquamarine waters. Seals loll in the translucent calm while pelicans on patrol glide overhead. Intoxicating air, brilliant sunshine, and bright yellow blooms kept me smiling in what is dubbed the "crown jewel of the state park system."

Point Lobos, or Point of the Sea Wolves, is just as gorgeous beneath the water as it is above. The Carmel submarine that lies just north of Point Lobos is a deep canyon that provides cold, nutrient-rich waters that fuel a vast array of marine life. Wildlife includes seals, sea lions, sea otters, and migrating gray whales. Thousands of shorebirds also make the reserve their home. Hiking trails follow the shoreline and lead across flower-laden meadows to hidden coves.

You must share the paths with hordes of tourists from around the globe, but I was able to leave the crowds by taking a stiff ascent up to Whaler's Knoll. I knew a panoramic view awaited me at the top because the whalers would go there to scan the entire bay on both sides of the knoll for whale spouts. So effective were they in the killing, they plundered the bounty almost to extinction. Whaler's Cove where the trial begins was once crimson with the blood of whales stacked in the bay. I found a glorious lunch spot beneath a ragged, wind-blown cypress that sheltered me from the intense sun.

The mile-long, white, sandy stretch at the Carmel River Beach beckoned in the distance. I took a stroll down the Carmel River State Beach that features a bird sanctuary in a lagoon just before the river empties into the sea. Nearby Carmel is a charming sea-side village with pricy art galleries and storybook homes sporting gardens bulging with blooms. Lunch at the Hog's Breath, owned by Clint Eastwood, is worth the wait. You can mosey on over to the elegant Doris Day's Hotel, a.k.a. Cypress Inn, and enjoy a brew at the English pub. Visitors and their pets are welcome at this legendary overnight oasis.

Point Lobos State Park
www.parks.ca.gov/?page_id=571

Hogs Breath Inn
www.hogsbreathinn.net/

Cypress Inn
www. cypress-inn.com/

(28) Rancho del Oso - Santa Cruz

Where Redwoods Meet The Sea

Waddell Beach is a wild stretch of surf eighteen miles north of Santa Cruz on Highway One. I was driving to San Francisco from L. A. when the rust-colored meadow with its muted mauve and lavender grasses lacing the winding, sea-bound creek called to me. Flashes of ducks, geese, and other shorebirds stirred my birding instincts. I yearned to know the valley that stretches from the beach into the redwood basin better.

Rancho del Oso Nature Preserve is an easy, wide trail that winds through beach, marsh, stream, and a riparian corridor. Self-guided trail maps can be easily obtained at the nature center about a half-mile into the park. Most hikers are content to take the lower trail from the beach up to Berry Creek Falls, felt by many to be the most beautiful falls in all of the Santa Cruz parks. Across from the falls is a platform with benches, affording fine views. The clever hiker can have a friend drop them off at the park headquarters at the top of Big Basin and hike about five hours down to Waddell Beach. An afternoon bus from Waddell Beach returns to Santa Cruz. Be sure to check times and schedules before making that commitment. The ambitious hiker may take the Skyline-to-the-Sea Trail thirteen miles to the top of the basin and enjoy extravagant vistas.

Big Basin is California's oldest state park, established in 1902 to save the ancient redwood forests. The park has grown to more than 18,000 acres with more than 80 miles of trails passing among streams, waterfalls, and old-growth redwoods. Redwoods were heavily logged in the basin by William Waddell from 1867 to 1875. Logging stopped when he was killed by a grizzly bear, and the valley became known as the canyon of the bear. Grizzly bears have not been seen in the area since the 1920s. In 1913, Theodore Hoover was able to buy much of the Waddell Creek watershed. His Rancho del Oso encompassed about 3,000 acres, reaching from the ocean to the boundary of Big Basin Redwoods State Park.

Since that time, five generations of his family have lived here. There are still private family homes bordering the parkland. I felt a twinge of envy as I strolled past the neatly-trimmed redwood homesteads of his descendants. The sun was smiling on their meadow, bright with yellow wildflowers, dotted with persimmon trees heavy with orange globes. Neat rows of purple cabbage and a variety of lettuces fanned the foothills. A thick hedge of berry bush brambles surrounded the fields to keep the deer and wild pigs from harvesting the crops.

I crossed a wooden bridge and walked beside Waddell Creek where the remains of a cement weir are used in the biological study of fish. During spring and winter months you may see mature steelhead and salmon in deep pools. President Hoover, an enthusiastic angler, fished here when he visited his brother. As a state park, the stream is now closed to fishing.

When I entered the deep redwood forest, the temperature dropped ten degrees. The cool breath of the towering monsters felt like a deep drink of soothing water. Lacy ferns nestled at the base of the trees, ensconced in brilliant green moss. A gauze of Spanish moss draped the upper limbs of the evergreens. Warblers flashed through the still forest, illuminated by beams of light streaming through the protective arms overhead. I strained to see the birds I heard chirping. A kingfisher, a red-tailed hawk fat from easy pickings, and the flash of a stellar jay were all I could see.

As I was leaving, a wedge of pelicans came in for a splash-landing in the estuary. Curlew poked for treats in the mud at low tide. I wanted to stay longer to explore more, but the fog was rolling in and it was time to go. I vowed to return to see the wildflowers in the spring and feel the cool forests in the summer. The constantly changing panorama of this natural wonderland is so varied that it demands the hiker return.

Guided walks are provided on the weekends by docents. A horse camp is available for equestrians who bring their own mounts. Along with the equestrian trails in the park are trails for hikers and bikers.

This a list of the hike options at **Rancho del Oso**.
www. bit.ly/2jbSraL

Big Basin Headquarters
www. bit.ly/2ikWjlB
21600 Big Basin Way in Boulder Creek 831-338-8860

(29) Jack London's Beauty Ranch Spared

About twenty years ago, I followed Billy and Saxon, characters in Jack London's novel, *The Valley of the Moon*, on their journey in a buckboard wagon up the coast of California on their search for the perfect place to land. They put down roots in what is now the Jack London Historic Park in Glen Ellen. Jack purchased the land in 1905 and dubbed it his "Beauty Ranch." In my essay, *Jack London and Me,* I detail how my life and that of the master of adventure-writing have intersected. I yearned to be closer to him and had to visit the haven he created and pay my respects to a man I admire and consider a kindred spirit.

At that time, there was a stable on the property and I rode horseback on the 20 miles veining 1,400 acres to the ridge of the Sonoma mountains through old-growth redwoods and madrones to the lake Jack created by building a dam.

He and his wife Charmian rode through the forests on sun-dappled days to the lake where they swam and dried off in the sun. He also built a bath house for guests to change. He enjoyed lively conversation and good company at the end of the day. He welcomed people from all walks of life to enjoy his Beauty Ranch, from literary luminaries to an ex-convict he knew from hard times.

On a recent visit, one month before flames from one of the largest fires in California history scorched nearby vineyards and destroyed over 6,000 homes, I hiked the trail to the lake that is now choked with reeds and algae. I was told the state of California does not have the resources to repair the dam and maintain the lake. Still, the mist rising from the forest floor and the sunbeams streaming through towering trees on my early morning walk around the lake were magical.

Jack is best known for his writing, but he was also an agrarian visionary. He purchased the land for his ranch from six farmers who had gone bankrupt because they had "worked the land out." Like many early farmers, they'd stripped the land of nutrients and then moved on to destroy the next plot they landed on. When he was a war correspondent in Korea in 1904, Jack learned how to retain moisture in the land by terracing. He studied farming, and used green and animal manures, nitrogen-gathering cover crops, and he rotated his crops to keep the soil alive. He gave two hours a day to his writing and ten to applying the most modern farming techniques to his ranch. Today, the rolling hills surrounding the structures on the property are planted with vines.

I was disturbed to learn that the Beauty Ranch is now run and maintained by volunteers. The state does not allocate funds to keep the ranch operational. Volunteer docents open the humble cottage where Jack and Charmian lived from

1905 until he died in 1916. The Wolf House, Jack's other big dream that he poured all his treasure and vital energies into, was a massive four-story structure of redwood timbers on a stone foundation designed to last. Just two days before the Londons were to move in, it burned beyond repair under mysterious circumstances. Jack, a dedicated socialist and defender of the common man, made many political enemies, but we can only guess what or who started this devastating blaze.

I have returned to the Beauty Ranch many times. I receive inspiration strolling in the shade of stately oak woodlands and towering redwoods. I always learn more about Jack in the House of Happy Walls Museum that Charmian had built to ensure people would not forget Jack's greatest vision— the Beauty Ranch he loved so well. I believe that "the secret to youth is to fill your mind with beauty." I always feel rejuvenated when I walk the paths on the land Jack restored to vibrant life.

During the fire raging through the wine country, docents rescued treasures Jack had gathered on his many exploits and his manuscripts from the cottage and the Happy House. For now, the Beauty Ranch remains for all of us to enjoy. The day I was there in September, workers were building a platform for an event scheduled to raise funds to keep the Beauty Ranch open to the public.

"The sunset fires, refracted from the cloud-driftage of the autumn sky, bathed the canyon with crimson, in which ruddy-limbed madrones and wine-wooded manzanitas burned and smoldered. The air was aromatic with laurel. Wild grapevines bridged the stream from tree to tree. Oaks of many sorts were veiled in lacy Spanish moss. Ferns and brakes grew lush beside the stream."

"I've got a hunch," said Billy.

"Let me say it first," Saxon begged.

He waited, his eyes on her face as she gazed about her in rapture.

"We've found our valley," she whispered. "Was that it?

~Jack London, *The Valley of the Moon*

Jack London Beauty Ranch
> www. jacklondonpark.com/jack-london-beauty-ranch. html

Note: You can still ride in the park by making an appointment with **TripleCreekHorseOutfitl.com**.
> www. triplecreekhorseoutfit.com/

Jack London and Me
> www.yourlifeisatrip.com/home/jack-london-and-me.html

(30) Point Reyes National Seashore

I hear the fog buoy, soft and low, rising from Tomales Bay. The sky is damp, gray, and cool. On my walk that took me past Muddy Hollow Pond beside the Limantour estuary, I spied the great white cranes in flight, a troop of pelicans, black cormorant, and more. Venturing further up a rise brought me to a meadow powdered with pink wildflowers that gently shifted in a refreshing breeze. Puffing to the top, I turned to face the vista of pale blue water spread out before me. Drakes Bay is skirted by a crescent of white sand. The estuary in the foreground is rich brown mud that becomes exposed with the fallen tide. Mounds of forest-green, mossy grass form the wetland floor. Pencil-legged cranes with flat, webbed feet stalk the nutrient-rich carpet for delectable tidbits.

When I approached the meadow, a regal hawk flew up from his nest. It landed on a strong limb that was low to the ground where it preened, its head turning to look straight at me with owl-like eyes. As I was leaving his meadow, the hawk actually dove at me, coming dangerously close with talons extended to let me know I was not welcome. I was startled to run into a stray Tule elk with a full rack of antlers grazing peacefully. Elk are known to be aggressive at times, but he seemed to take no interest in me.

In *The Mindful Hiker,* Stephen Altschuler has a love affair with the Sky Trail in Point Reyes National Park. He shares what it means to be totally in the present, listening, smelling, seeing, and contemplating your surroundings as you put one foot in front of the other. Walking this trail, he finds solace, inspiration, equilibrium, and peace. He makes reference to soulful thinkers he has met and/or read in his life, and quotes them liberally. As a counselor, he has dealt with his own grief, as well as the confusion and grief of others. His walks on Sky Trail have been his salvation. I found this book to be a reminder of all the reasons I need to hike alone at times. The chinchilla-wheel of thought stops turning, the stream runs clean, and I am free to be again. *The Mindful Hiker* reminds us we can find peace if we open our hearts and minds to receive the bounty in nature.

Stop at the Bear Valley Visitor Bureau to pick up a map and check road closures. Limantour Road takes you to the easy walks on Muddy Hollow Trail, Limantour spit and Estero Trail. Sir Francis Drake Boulevard takes you deeper into the park to wind-blown Drakes Beach and the historic Point Reyes lighthouse, I could spend many days roaming the vast network of trails in this splendid preserve.

If you like to shuck fresh oysters, stop in nearby Tomales Bay and try the Hog Island Oyster Company. For more generic fare, try the Cowgirl Cantina. They offer picnic fixings, salads, sandwiches, cheese, and sausage and more to go.

Point Reyes National Seashore
www.nps.gov/pore/index.htm

Hog Island Oyster Company
www. hogislandoysters.com/

(31) Russian River Road - Armstrong Redwood Forest

The cool breath of the redwood forest nestled halfway between Santa Rosa and the Pacific Ocean on the Russian River Road greeted me as I entered the Armstrong Reserve. Light streams though the arms of the giants spotlighting ferns that frame an energetic creek charging through the forest. It rains as much as 55 inches a year here, plus the morning fog keeps the primeval forest floor damp and cool. The majestic trees that tower overhead were spared the axe by timberman Colonel James Armstrong in the 1870s. It is one of the last remaining groves of coastal redwood trees in California that can live to be 2,000 years old. The mystical forest encourages reflection and somber thoughts as you consider that these trees have survived centuries of change and upheaval. The Pioneer Nature Trail is an easy amble that winds though the shady park, but there are a host of trails with varying degrees of difficulty to explore.

There are numerous casual eateries in nearby Guerneville, but why not make it a fabulous day and take the scenic River Road all the way to the coast? A lovely way to cap off this is day is a repast at the River's End Lodge where the Russian River meets the ocean blue. If you are really lucky, you can stay in one of the four cabins perched on the bluff overlooking a full-blown sea.

After a sumptuous seafood lunch, I leaned into the brisk wind and plodded through deep sand to a spit called Goat Rock. A colony of fur and leopard seals lie basking on the sandy spit. There was an upswell of fur and flesh as they *galumphed* over the sand to safer waters when I got close. One pup rolled over onto his back and stared at me with liquid brown eyes. Others scampered into the icy water

Upon leaving the beach, I spotted trails lacing the bluffs along Highway One that hugs the coast. They called to me for another visit to this beautiful region one fine day.

Armstrong Park
www.parks.ca.gov/?page_id=450

Note: The reserve is located three miles north of Guerneville on Armstrong Woods Road. From Highway 101, take the River Road exit (in Santa Rosa). Go west on River Road until you reach Guerneville. At the second stop light, make a right hand turn onto Armstrong Woods Road.

River's End Lodge and Restaurant
www.ilovesunsets.com/home.html

(32) Russian Gulch Waterfall - Nature's Give-Away

In Russian Gulch State Park south of Mendocino, a shady, well-groomed trail takes you to a sparkling cascade in a fern grotto. The 5-mile roundtrip hike tracing Little River in

Van Damme Park is easily accessed and winds up a lush canyon to a pigmy forest.

A man who looked like a gnome greeted me from the shadows of Fern Canyon where the path had been washed out in hard winter rains. He was sitting peacefully on a cushion he'd brought on a bench beneath the giant redwood trees that dwell in this water-rich valley. He was reading a book written in French, not because he is, but because he likes the writer. He wore a jaunty hat, gloves, khaki pants, and a tan sweatshirt with a button-down collar. He told me he lived in Orange County for twenty years before coming here. Each day, he hikes into these woods to know their quiet. He said it was like going to church every day. He directed me to the waterfall. I thanked him for the tip and felt a sense of mysterious guidance as I carried on.

Life-giving oxygen to the brain refreshing the senses is nature's "give-away." Vibrant green moss hugs the trunks of giant redwoods, keeping the walk cool. Lacy plants clamor to the top of the canyon wall, leaving their children behind. Delicate maidenhair ferns sprout beneath their shady cover. The path is lined with thick layers of devil's club, a grand, green bouquet with a few bobbing heads of red columbine to brighten the scene.

There are numerous other trails and hiking ops in the region, but this is my favorite. The birding is phenomenal, especially along Big River where the hike delivers you. You may rent a kayak and paddle with the incoming tide to see herons, egrets, osprey, and more. If you continue on the left fork, you will arrive at a 36-foot waterfall in .07 miles. If you take the right fork, the Falls Loop Trail, you'll go up and over a ridge and arrive at the same destination in 1.6 miles. The reward for the longer route is a greater variety of habitats and the thought that you have earned your lunch in nearby Mendocino.

The village of Mendocino boasts gussied-up, turn-of-the-century Victorian cottages painted bright colors with window boxes sporting bright blooms. The gardening competition here is intense, with each home topping the next in a fussy profusion of flowers. There are art galleries from high- to low-brow, but the best deals are at the Mendocino Art Center on Little River Street where local artists display their wares at favorable prices.

The weather here is intoxicating. Peerless blue skies with mist hanging over the Mendocino headlands call for a stroll on the bluffs. I walked above scalloped coves where I actually saw a swimmer doing the backstroke. He looked like a lone fly in a giant jade-green punchbowl, fringed with white lace. A soft breeze off the sea kept me cool me from the warming sun.

At the Trillium Inn, the chef ran out to clip some fresh herbs from a glorious garden sporting indigenous plants. Matilija poppies with white crepe petals and yellow snowball centers swayed on tall stalks in the breeze. Giant red hollyhocks and purple plumes of Mexican sage added color to the greens. My summer salad arrived, topped with the juiciest, most flavorful tomatoes I have ever tasted.

Trillium Inn
> www. trilliummendocino.com/

Russian Gulch State Park
> www.parks.ca.gov/?page_id=432

Additional Resources

This book is intended to capture the essence of each outdoor day listed. For more specific information, including maps of the trails, this a list of good resources:

*All Trails is a digital resource that lists trails all over the United States. The annual subscription is worth the fee if you intend to do a lot of hiking. There are peer reviews to help you gauge the difficulty of the hike and maps that can be downloaded to your phone. www.alltrails.com/

*Robert Stone is the author of numerous day-hike collections specific to several of the areas I spotlight. *Day Hikes in Santa Barbara, Monterey and Carmel* and *Ventura* and more are available in print online and in bookstores. www.amazon.com/

The Complete Hiker's Guide to the Backbone Trail compiled by Doug & Caroline Chamberlin is a must-have if you are thinking about doing the entire 69 miles of the Backbone. However, they break the trail down into segments which is very handy for day-hikers.
https://www.amazon.com/Complete-Hikers-Guide-Backbone-Trail/dp/0997957700/

Walkabout Northern California-Hiking Inn to Inn by Tom Courtney is a wonderful resource for those in need of extended hikes. Footpaths by day, with cozy lodging at the end of long hiking day, are commonplace in England but seemingly rare in California. Courtney puts an end to that misconception with this book. www.amazon.com/

*John McKinney, a.k.a. the **"Trail Master"** has a host of hike books on his site. His mini-pocket guides are easy to slip into your pack. www.thetrailmaster.com/

More Books by Linda Ballou

Lost Angel Walkabout-One Traveler's Tales

Awaken your senses with thrilling tales of an intrepid soul's search for beauty in the wilds. Linda Ballou embraces life and draws readers into her adventures with vivid descriptions that make you feel as if you are traveling beside her.
 www.amazon.com

For more of Linda's travel adventures go to:
www.LostAngelAdventures.com.

The Cowgirl Jumped Over the Moon

There's heartbreak, deceit, courage, loss, and redemption. And yes, there's romance. From the glamorous world of California showjumping to the freedom of riding the trails in the John Muir Wilderness. The descriptions make you feel you are there. www.amazon.com and www.audible.com

Wai-nani: A Voice from Old Hawai'i

Be transported to magical old Hawai'i. Precocious Wai-nani's character is inspired by the powerful personage of Ka'ahumanu, the favorite wife of Kamehameha the Great. He united the islands and gave his people a golden age. By hi side, she rose to become the most powerful woman in old Hawai'i. www.amazon.com and www.audible.com

Sign up for Linda's Blog posts at:
 www.LindaBallouTalkingToYou.blogspot.com/

To learn more about Linda's books go to:
www.LindaBallouAuthor.com